DATE DUE

J

[

JUN

CASEY!

THE SPORTS CAREER OF CHARLES STENGEL

BY:

JAMES & LYNN HAHN

EDITED BY:

DR. HOWARD SCHROEDER

Professor in Reading and Language Arts
Dept. of Elementary Education
Mankato State University

CRESTWOOD HOUSE

Mankato, Minnesota

CIP

LIBRARY OF CONGRESS CATALOGING IN PUBLICATION DATA
Hahn, James.
    Casey! The sports career of Charles Stengel.

    (Sports legends)
    SUMMARY: A brief biography of the baseball manager whose team, the
New York Yankees, won five World Series in a row.
    1. Stengel, Casey — Juvenile literature. 2. Baseball managers — United
States — Biography — Juvenile literature. 3. New York (City). Baseball Club
(American League) — Juvenile literature. [1. Stengel, Casey. 2. Baseball
managers] I. Hahn, Lynn, joint author. II. Schroeder, Howard. III. Title. IV.
Series.
GV865.S8H34   796.357'092'4   [B]   [92]   80-28602
ISBN 0-89686-126-0 (lib. bdg.)
ISBN 0-89686-141-4 (pbk.)

INTERNATIONAL STANDARD BOOK NUMBERS	LIBRARY OF CONGRESS CATALOG CARD NUMBERS
0-89686-126-0 Library Bound	80-28602
0-89686-141-4 Paperback	

PHOTO CREDITS:

Cover: Focus on Sports, Inc.

FPG: 3, 16-17, 31, 35
UPI: 5, 7, 21B, 23, 24-25, 27, 28, 29, 34, 39, 40, 42,
    43, 45
Bettmann Archives: 10, 14, 19, 32-33
Culver Pictures: 21A
Wide World Photos: 37, 38

CRESTWOOD HOUSE

Crestwood House, Inc., Box 3427, Hwy. 66 So., Mankato, MN 56001

CASEY!

CHAPTER 1

Casey Stengel was one of baseball's best managers. From 1949 to 1960, he managed the New York Yankees and won ten American League pennants and seven World Series'. Casey was the only manager to win five World Series' in a row.

Before becoming a manager, Casey played major league baseball. From 1912 to 1923, he played the outfield for such National League teams as Brooklyn, Pittsburgh, Philadelphia, New York, and Boston. As a major league manager, he also led Brooklyn (1934-1936), Boston (1938-1943), and the New York Mets (1962-1965).

What an amazing man! How did he do it all? Casey Stengel's story begins when he was born on July 30, 1890 in Kansas City, Missouri. He was named Charles Dillon Stengel. Casey's mother, Jennie, was Irish and his father, Louis, was German.

Casey's father sold insurance and also sprayed water on the dusty streets. He used a water wagon with a wooden water tank pulled by horses. Casey said his mother cooked the best meals in the neighborhood. He enjoyed her homemade catsup, jams and jellies. His mom's gravy also pleased him. "I

Team owners and Casey celebrate after the Yankees had won the World Series for the fifth year in a row. No other manager or team has ever equaled that record.

used to take that big gravy spoon," Casey said, "and put it in those mashed potatoes. And I'd flap them down on the plate. Then get a good steak and put it on top of that."

For dessert, Casey said she was, "great on lemon pie. She would buy two lemons and make them go a long way. We'd have lemon pie maybe once a month. In those days it was hard to get lemons in Missouri."

Casey first attended Woodland Grade School

and later Garfield Grade School. At Woodland Grade School, everyone had to write right-handed. As a left-hander, Casey didn't want to change. His teacher kept him after school. She made him stand in a closet for half an hour until he started writing right-handed.

When he got older, Casey was glad his teacher had made him write right-handed. After being an awkward kid, Casey said he became a good baseball player because he could use his right hand so well. He batted with his left, used his left hand to throw, and his right to catch. Casey said he could use his right hand better than most lefties because he had learned to write right-handed.

As a boy, Casey's blond hair and blue eyes earned him the nickname, "Dutch." After school he played baseball on vacant lots. Casey had fun playing baseball. Once, he and his brother, Grant, used a potato for a trick play. Casey was pitching. Grant was playing shortstop. Grant hid a baseball-sized potato in his hip pocket. After failing to tag a runner out at second base, Grant threw the potato, instead of the ball, back to Casey. Later, when the runner stepped off the base to take a lead, Grant tagged him out with the ball. The other team was so angry they chased Casey and Grant home.

Casey and his brother played another game called "shinny." They flattened a tin can, and then hit it with sticks. He also roller skated a lot. Since there weren't any ballbearings in his roller skates, he took grease from the cables that pulled the cable cars in the streets of Kansas City. He greased his skates to make them go faster.

Daily chores were a part of Casey's youth. He had to wash the dishes and take care of their cow. Since Casey's father enjoyed milk, Casey and his brother had to milk the cow. Casey wasn't a good milker, so he kept the flies away with a stick while his brother milked. When they had extra milk, Casey and his brother sold it to neighbors.

Casey in his early days as a baseball player.

As a member of St. Mark's Episcopal Church, Casey earned twenty-five cents on Sundays for working the pump on the organ.

Whenever Casey had extra money, he bought ice cream sundaes and candy. He also went downtown to Kansas City to watch vaudeville shows. At Keith's Theater, he enjoyed laughing at the comedians on stage.

At Kansas City Central High School, Casey played every team sport. In 1906 he played fullback on the football team. His teammates elected him captain in 1909. Casey played on the basketball team from 1908 through 1910. He helped his team win the state championship.

Sports didn't take all Casey's time. One day he made a date with a girl named Margolis. He had to meet her mother and father before he could take her out. While getting dressed for his date, Casey saw that his shoes were old and worn. So, he decided to wear his brother's new patent leather shoes.

Although Casey's feet were too big for the shoes, he kept trying to put them on. He pulled and pulled, and finally made it. While trying, he had grabbed one shoe's tongue and pulled so hard it had come off. He taped the tongue back on with some black tape.

While Casey was talking with Margolis' parents, the tight shoes started to hurt him. Looking down, he saw the tongue had slipped off. He crossed his feet to hide the tongue. Then, he couldn't sit still because his feet got cramps.

Finally, Casey jumped up and ran home. He taped the tongue on again and hid the shoes in the closet. A few days later, his brother found the shoes and started a fight with Casey. The fight ended when Grant ran away and Casey couldn't catch him.

CHAPTER 2

Casey's baseball career was just starting. Baseball was Casey's favorite sport. He hit the ball hard, ran fast, and had a strong arm. He played third base, outfield, and pitcher. *THE CENTRALIAN,* his high school yearbook, said, "the baseball team was strong in every way, with the feature being the hurling of Stengel."

The baseball team elected Casey captain in 1908. In the spring of 1909, he pitched in the state championship against Joplin, Missouri. Casey pitched for fifteen innings and Central High won, 7-6.

During the summers of 1908 and 1909, Casey played baseball for the Kansas City Red Sox, a semi-pro team. They'd travel twenty-five to seventy-five

Young Casey takes a practice swing.

miles every day. In country hotels, Casey sometimes played jokes on his teammates. He'd put pieces of rubber hose in their beds to make them think there were snakes.

Baseball scouts from the Kansas City Blues, a minor league team, watched Casey play. They thought he played well, so they signed him to play for them after he graduated in 1910.

Kid Nichols, Casey said, gave him the best advice before he started playing for the Blues. Kid was a great pitcher who's now in baseball's Hall of Fame. Kid told Casey, "When you start out in baseball, the best thing you can do is listen to your manager. And once in a while you'll have an older player teach you. Never say, 'I won't do that.' Always listen to him. If you're not going to do it, don't tell him so. Let it go in one ear and roll around there for a month. Then, if it isn't any good, let it go out the other ear. If it is good, memorize and keep it. Now be sure you do that and you'll keep out of trouble."

When Casey started playing for the Kansas City Blues he weighed one hundred and sixty-five pounds and was five feet eleven inches tall. The pros hit his pitching, and he had trouble fielding balls hit off the walls. The manager decided Casey wasn't good enough to play for the Blues. He sent Casey to a team in Kankakee, Illinois to learn more about baseball. Casey earned $135 a month there, and lived in a rooming house for four dollars a week. For $3.50, he bought a meal ticket at McBroom's Restaurant. "You could," Casey said, "go a long way on that." Occasionally he got invited to someone's house for dinner.

The Kankakee team lost money and went out of business. Casey went to a team in Shelbyville, Kentucky in the Blue Grass League. After that team went out of business, Casey played for a team in Maysville, Kentucky. There, many fans and players called him a "clown." After catching fly balls during pre-game practice, Casey would throw the ball to second base and his glove toward the infield. Then, he would run toward his glove and slide into it. Casey said he was just practicing catching, throwing, running and sliding at the same time.

Casey would do anything to catch a fly ball. A stream flowed behind the outfield at Maysville. Once, running back to catch a fly ball, Casey ran into the stream. While standing in the stream, he caught the ball.

CHAPTER 3

Although Casey liked baseball, he still wasn't sure he wanted to make it his career. After the baseball season, he went to Western Dental College in Kansas City, Missouri. Casey had a hard time learning how to be a dentist. One day his teacher asked him to pull a patient's tooth. The patient was very tall and Casey didn't set the chair low enough. No matter how hard Casey pulled and twisted, the tooth wouldn't come out. He yanked it so hard, he almost pulled the patient out of the chair. Finally, Casey's teacher stopped him, shouting, "You're left-handed! You're left-handed!"

At that time, dental tools were made only for right-handers. Casey said he did everything right except switching hands. The next spring Casey left dental school and went back to baseball.

In the spring of 1912, Casey played for the Brooklyn Dodgers' minor league team in Montgomery, Alabama. There, many more people called him a "clown."

Before one game, he saw a manhole cover in the outfield. Looking inside, he saw the hole was only a few feet deep. During the game, he crawled down into the hole. Then, he lifted the cover up just enough to see where the ball was hit. Soon, a batter hit a ball towards Casey. Holding the manhole cover like a shield, he jumped up. The fans gasped while Casey struggled with the heavy cover. Staggering around, he caught the ball and bowed while the fans cheered.

Despite his jokes, Casey was the best player on that team. In September, 1912, the Dodgers called him up to the major leagues. Casey got lost at the Dodger's ball park in Brooklyn. He couldn't find the players' door. He told an usher he was a rookie and asked for directions.

"The clubhouse is down there," the usher said, "and you'd better be good!"

In the clubhouse, he got his nickname. A player asked where he was from and Casey said, "Kansas City."

"K.C.," the player said. "We'll call you Casey from now on."

Casey was better than good in his first major league game. He hit a single his first time at bat. Then he slugged three more hits and stole two bases. "Casey Stengel is the new Ty Cobb," news-

Casey slams another hit for the Brooklyn Dodgers!

papers said the next day. Ty Cobb was one of the best baseball players ever. Later, Casey said, "Pretty soon they found out I was nothing but old Casey Stengel."

In six seasons with the Brooklyn Dodgers, Casey played well. In 1918, though, the Dodgers needed pitching help, so they traded him to the Pittsburgh Pirates.

Casey still liked to act like a clown. When the Pirates played their first game of the 1918 season in Brooklyn, the Dodger fans booed Casey. Since he was on the other team, they didn't like him. In the second inning, before stepping into the batter's box, Casey tipped his hat to the fans. A sparrow flew out. The fans laughed, and their jeers became cheers.

Casey only played with the Pirates for two years. He argued with the team's owner about his pay. In one game, Casey took too much time chasing a fly ball. The fans booed. "What do you expect," Casey yelled at them, "from a fella who's starving to death?" The team's owner didn't like that, so he traded Casey to the Philadelphia Phillies.

At Philadelphia, Casey played well until injuring his back in 1921. Then he was traded to the New York Giants. One day a pitched ball almost hit Casey's head. Casey fought with the pitcher until two policemen led him from the field.

Casey learned to control his temper and helped

the Giants win pennants in 1921, 1922, and 1923. In the 1923 World Series, the Giants played the Yankees. Although Casey hit two home runs, the Yankees won the Series.

As a Giant, Casey learned a lot about baseball

In this team picture of the 1922 Giants, Casey is third from the left in the second row.

from John McGraw, a great manager. Twenty-five years later, he would use what he'd learned to manage the New York Yankees.

In 1924, the Giants wanted younger players, so they traded Casey to the Boston Braves. That was a

happy year for Casey. He played well for Boston and married Edna Lawson. After the wedding, Casey told reporters, "It was the best catch I ever made."

Casey's major league playing career ended in the spring of 1925, but his managing career was just beginning. The Brave's owner hired him as president and manager of a minor league team in Worcester, Massachusetts.

In 1925, Casey managed Worcester to a third place finish. During the winter, he was asked to manage a better team in Toledo, Ohio. He asked his Boston boss if he could take the job. After his boss said no, Casey planned a clever move. As president of the Worcester team, Casey wrote a letter to himself, firing his manager, Casey Stengel. Then, Casey quit his president's job and went to Toledo.

Casey managed the Toledo Mudhens for six seasons. During that time he learned more about directing players and winning ball games. In 1927, Casey led the Mudhens to first place and the "Little World Series" title.

In 1931, Casey wanted to get back into the major leagues. He applied for a coaching job with the Brooklyn Dodgers. He was hired, and for two years taught the Dodgers how to play better. Although the Dodgers lost many games, Casey was hired to manage the team in 1934 for $12,000 per year.

The Dodgers respected Casey and played well

His years as manager of the Dodgers were often frustrating for Casey.

for him. Casey advised and taught without shouting or cursing. Instead of poking fun at their weaknesses, he praised their strengths. When a player broke the rules and gave an excuse, Casey said, "I used that old story ten years ago as a player. Better get another one next time." The Dodgers, loyal to Casey, tried hard to win for him.

After the Dodgers knocked the Giants out of the 1934 pennant race, the fans carried Casey onto the subway and rode for hours singing and dancing.

Casey wanted to win more games for Brooklyn. He worked many hours to improve as a manager. He had his players practice batting in the morning. In the afternoon, he taught them how to run bases and bunt better. He even invented the pick-off play where the pitcher turns and throws back to second base.

Although Casey managed well, the Dodgers had a bad season and he was fired in 1936. "A man does the best he can," Casey told reporters. "The players tried hard enough. They just didn't have it."

"Casey is a good manager," Clark Griffith, the Washington Senators' owner, told reporters. "No one could have done as much with that Brooklyn team he had to manage."

"He knows baseball," said Sid Mercer, a writer for the JOURNAL-AMERICAN newspaper. "Casey can handle men."

The Boston Braves thought Casey could manage their team, so they hired him in 1938. Casey tried to win games with old, lazy players and young, unskilled players. With Boston for six years, Casey didn't win many games. In the spring of 1943, a speeding car hit him, breaking his leg. Although he

Casey gets into another argument, and loses.

gio's crowding thirty-five. Tommy Henrich is thirty-six. They'll be lucky to finish third behind the Cleveland Indians and the Boston Red Sox."

Casey didn't want to finish in third place. During spring training he made his players practice every morning and afternoon. He worked them ten to twelve hours every day. Casey worked fifteen hours a day, studying other teams. He wanted to find their strong and weak points.

During the season, Casey platooned his players. Instead of using the same player in the same

Casey got so mad about an opponent's player not being called out at home, that he had a series of photos enlarged to prove his point.

place every game, he moved them around. He used different players for different games. For example, in place of the injured DiMaggio, he used Hank Bauer and Gene Woodling. He used Bauer against left-handed pitchers, and Woodling for right-handers. Casey also worked on his players' timing, teaching them how to hit the ball to opposite fields.

Luck didn't favor Casey that year. The Yankees had fifteen injuries in April, thirteen in May, and seventy-six during the season. Somehow, Casey kept his team in first. Then, in September, Boston

caught and passed the Yankees. With just two games left in the season, the Red Sox had a one game lead. To win the pennant, the Yankees had to win both games. Each game was against Boston.

Casey didn't sleep the night before the first game. He paced the floor, thinking and making plans for the game. His plans paid off when the Yankees won the first game, 5-4.

The next night, Casey again stayed up. He wrote twelve different lineups for the game. Then he tore them up. He wrote twelve more lineups, moving and switching players around. He tore them up, too. Finally, he chose one lineup, and the Yankees won with it. In the World Series, Casey led the Yankees over the Brooklyn Dodgers.

In November, 1949, one hundred and sixteen reporters voted for "Manager of the Year." One hundred and one voted for Casey Stengel.

"Casey was lucky last year," reporters said in the spring of 1950. "He was a magician, pulling rabbits out of a top hat. This year Boston is better and so is Cleveland." Most writers picked the Yankees to finish in third place.

"The Yankees are full of old men," reporters said. Casey used those "old men" to win ball games. Throughout the 1950 season, those "old men" played hard for Casey every minute. They understood his great baseball knowlege. Casey knew just when to put in the right player and take out the

Casey passes the time with Yankee catcher, Yogi Berra, as they wait for a new pitcher to come in.

wrong one. His moves won many games.

After the Yankees clinched the pennant on September 29, 1950, reporters said Casey was lucky again. Proving them wrong, Casey led the Yankees over the Philadelphia Phillies in four games to win the World Series. For a reward, the Yankees raised his pay to $85,000 per year.

In the spring of 1951, Casey decided he needed a few new players. He called Gil McDougald, twenty-two years old, up from the minor leagues. Casey taught him how to run, bunt, and pull the ball in the major leagues. Gil learned much from Casey and was the best hitter on the team that year. Casey also brought Mickey Mantle to the Yankees that season. After several games, Casey saw that Mickey needed to learn more. He sent Mickey down to the minor leagues. Near the end of the season, Casey recalled Mickey, and his thirteen home runs helped the Yankees win another pennant.

In the 1951 World Series, the Yankees played a tough New York Giant team. Planning carefully, Casey calmed his pitchers and advised his hitters. His managing skills won the Series. The Yankees shouldn't have won, but they did. Reporters voted Casey "Manager of the Year" again.

Two Yankee stars, Al Lopat (left) and Joe DiMaggio, share a piece of the manager's birthday cake.

Second baseman Billy Martin gets a big hug after the Yankees won the 1952 American League Pennant.

Although the Yankees had just won three World Series in a row, reporters still didn't pick them to win the flag in 1952. Since DiMaggio had retired and others were in the army, they said Casey didn't have a strong team.

Again, Casey proved the experts wrong. Juggling his players, he changed his lineup every day. When players made mistakes, he yelled at them. Casey said they'd better play well or be traded. On September 26, Casey's Yankees clinched their fourth American League title in a row. Finally, writers wrote, "Casey is the best manager ever."

Casey was winning with players who weren't supposed to win. He won despite hurt players and old stars. He won because he taught players how to win, and how to gain the will to win. In October, Casey's Yankees won their fourth straight World Series.

In 1953, Casey became the first manager to lead a team to five straight pennants. Then, when the Yankees beat the Dodgers in the World Series, he became the first manager to win five straight World Series.

CHAPTER 5

During the 1954 season, Casey had problems with his team. More players were called into the army and others were traded. Then, Mickey Mantle slipped into a hitting slump. Casey worked with Mickey every day, showing him how to watch the ball and swing. Despite Casey's moves, the Yankees didn't win enough. That year the Cleveland Indians won the American League Championship.

"The Yankees and Casey are finished," writers said. Working more hours that winter, Casey made several trades. His deals paid off when the Yankees won their sixth pennant. In the World Series, the Yankees lost to the Dodgers in seven games.

Casey didn't like losing the World Series for the first time. In 1956, he stayed up late at night, figuring out ways to win. He must have found the right answer, because the Yankees won the pennant again and beat the Dodgers in the 1956 World Series.

The Yankees won because Casey platooned his players. He used just the right player in the right place at the right time. He switched shortstops to outfielders. He changed second basemen to third basemen. He made third basemen first basemen, and catchers outfielders. Casey knew his players better then they knew themselves. They couldn't

Casey motions for a change.

Casey, Danny Thomas (center), and Manager Haney of the Braves meet the press before the start of the 1957 World Series.

see their own strengths and weaknesses like Casey did.

In the 1957 season, for example, Casey told Tony Kubek to play five different positions. Injuries forced Casey to change his lineup several times in a

game. Casey's moves worked and his team won its eighth flag. In the World Series, though, the Milwaukee Braves beat the Yankees in seven games.

Since Casey was sixty-eight years old, some people said he should retire. They said he was getting too old to manage the Yankees to their ninth pennant in 1958. After the Braves had a three game to one lead in the World Series, Casey directed the Yankees to win three games in a row. That was the seventh time Casey led the Yankees to win the World Series.

Some people said Casey should quit a winner. They didn't want old age to make him a loser. Casey signed a two year contract in 1959 and told reporters, "I will manage for twenty-two more years and then I'll buy the ball club." Many people

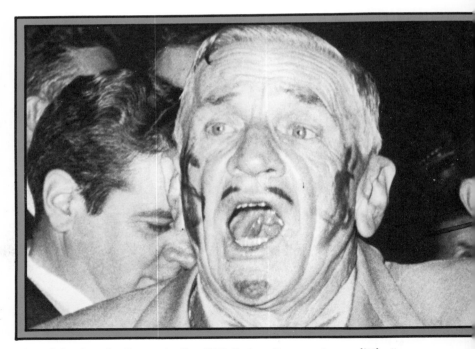

After defeating the Braves in the 1958 Series, Casey put on a little "war-paint!"

Casey and his wife headed for their home in California after he signed a new two-year contract.

laughed, but Casey kept on talking. "Baseball is my life. If I quit, what would I do? Sit by my swimming pool and watch games on television? Pick flaws in the way the other guys run their games? Baseball is excitement. It's drama. It's contest and struggle. Sure, I guess there comes a time when you retire. But you don't like to see it come."

After the 1959 season, more people said Casey should retire. Although he had the same players, who won the World Series the year before, they finished third. Reporters said Casey didn't manage correctly. The facts proved them wrong. The players didn't hit or pitch well. "The bat boy had a great year," Casey told reporters, "but he was the only one who did."

In 1960, during spring training, Casey made his players practice more. He drilled the Yankees in basic skills. He yelled, "We lost too many games last year by sloppy playing." Then he spoke in a way many reporters called "Stengelese." "You ain't gonna see much of that this year, I can tell you." So Casey, with sixty years of experience, taught his team how to run, slide, hit, and throw better.

Casey didn't accept poor play. Once, in August, Mickey Mantle was too lazy to run out a ground ball. Casey yanked him out of the game and made him sit on the bench. After that, Mantle and the other Yankees played harder and better. They won nineteen out of twenty-two games. Then they won the last fifteen games of the season to win the pennant. Reporters praised Casey for his skill as a manager.

The 1960 World Series was one of the most exciting ever. After six games, the Pittsburgh Pirates and the New York Yankees had each won three games. In the last half of the tenth inning of the seventh game, Bill Mazeroski hit a home run to win it for Pittsburgh.

After the Series, the Yankees held a press conference. "We all think Casey is the greatest manager in baseball," a Yankee owner said. "But he is seventy. The rigors of managing a team that must win every year are too much for a man of seventy. We cannot wait until an emergency arises. We have to

A disappointed Casey tells the press that he has just been fired because of his age.

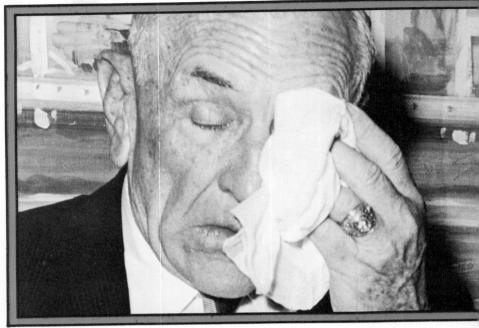

Casey broke down at a farewell party given by the baseball writers in New York. "Casey rained out," the press said.

bring in a younger man now."

As tears filled his eyes, Casey said, "I was told my services would no longer be required. I'll never make the mistake of being seventy again."

CHAPTER 6

Many fans, players, and reporters said Casey was treated unfairly. Baseball teams in Chicago, Detroit, and Los Angeles offered him jobs. Casey said he wanted to rest and think for a while.

Casey didn't rest and think for too many months. On September 29, 1961 he became the manager of baseball's newest team, the New York Mets. Since the Mets were a new team, they didn't have many good players. Casey spent hours planning to win games. Still, the Mets won only forty and lost one hundred and twenty. After the Mets

Reporters question Casey after he was hired to manage the Mets.

39

As manager of the "Amazin' Mets," Casey gave the fans what they liked to see!

For good luck, Casey was presented with a floral horseshoe on opening day in New York.

finished in tenth place, Casey said, "It was worse than I expected."

The Mets didn't improve, no matter what Casey said or did. Although the Mets finished in tenth place in 1963 and 1964, thousands of fans packed Shea Stadium. They enjoyed watching Casey lead his "Amazin' Mets" and argue with the umpires.

Suddenly, Casey Stengel's baseball career ended. On July 24, 1965, he fell while getting out of a taxi and broke his hip. A few days later, he told reporters, "I am not capable of walking out on the ball field. It's not proper for me to limp out there. I can't run out to take a pitcher out of the box. I don't want to complete my term." With tears in his eyes, Casey said that's all he had to say.

Baseball's greatest manager would never lead a team again.

Casey didn't stay away from baseball. In the spring of 1966, while he was watching the Mets, the Baseball Writers' Association of America had a special election. They voted Casey Stengel into the Hall of Fame. Thrilled, Casey limped around the grandstands, telling people, "If you didn't know, they just put me in the Hall of Fame."

During the party at the Hall of Fame, Casey gave a long speech. At the end, he said, "I want to thank my parents for letting me play baseball. And, I'm thankful I had baseball knuckles and couldn't become a dentist."

After being honored at the Hall of Fame, Casey attended many Met and Yankee Old Timers' games. He talked with the players, giving advice and tips.

As he got older, Casey still liked to talk about

baseball. Even sickness couldn't keep him quiet. In 1974, a sore throat kept him in the hospital for several days. When he got out, he told reporters, "The doctors say I ain't allowed to talk." Then he talked for an hour about his throat and his seventy years in baseball.

Casey never lost his sense of humor. During the 1975 Met's Old Timers' Day at Shea Stadium, reporters asked about his trip from California. "Don't ask about my trip," he laughed, "ask about my body." Later that year, he was too sick to attend the Yankees' Old Timers' Day.

On September 30, 1975, Casey Stengel died from cancer. He was eighty-five years old.

Fans, players, and reporters were sad to hear about his death. Maury Allen, a *NEW YORK POST* writer, said Casey was "a force of energy, a happening, a steamroller of excitement and vigor. He loved life. He loved it with a passion that consumed him. He loved the game of baseball."

After hearing Casey died, Mickey Mantle said, "He was like a father to me."

"He was wonderful," Joe DiMaggio said. "He understood his players and knew what to do with the talent he had."

"Casey Stengel had the mind of a genius," Hugh Carey, Governor of New York, said. "He had the heart of Santa Claus and St. Francis, and the face of a clown. Something very special has gone from

Even after he retired, Casey kept up an interest in the Mets. Here he gives the "go get 'em" sign after the Mets got into their first World Series in 1969.

At an Old Timer's Day, Casey reenacts a scene from his days as a young player, when he released a sparrow from under his cap during a league game.

our lives."

"He made more fans for baseball," Bowie Kuhn, baseball's Commissioner said, "than any other man who ever lived."

And, finally, a newspaper printed a story that ended. "Well, God is certainly getting an earful tonight."

IF YOU ENJOYED THIS STORY, THERE ARE MORE LEGENDS TO READ ABOUT: